Values

ILLUSTRATED SCRIPTURES
FOR LATTER-DAY SAINT YOUNG WOMEN

RYAN D. WALKER

RYAN
design
works, inc.

ISBN 978-0615528243

FOR AMY

Before
I formed thee in
the belly I knew thee;
and before thou camest
forth out of the womb
I sanctified thee, and
I ordained thee...

Jeremiah 1:5

AND NOW, AS YE ARE DESIROUS TO COME INTO THE FOLD OF GOD, AND TO BE CALLED HIS PEOPLE, AND ARE WILLING TO BEAR ONE ANOTHER'S BURDENS, THAT THEY MAY BE LIGHT; YEA, AND ARE WILLING TO MOURN WITH THOSE THAT MOURN; YEA, AND COMFORT THOSE THAT STAND IN NEED OF COMFORT, AND **TO STAND AS WITNESSES OF GOD AT ALL TIMES AND IN ALL THINGS, AND IN ALL PLACES** THAT YE MAY BE IN, EVEN UNTIL DEATH, THAT YE MAY BE REDEEMED OF GOD, AND BE NUMBERED WITH THOSE OF THE FIRST RESURRECTION, THAT YE MAY HAVE ETERNAL LIFE—

MOSIAH 18:8-9

Now faith is the substance of things hoped for, the evidence of things not seen.

—Hebrews 11:1

AND NOW AS I SAID CONCERNING

Faith

FAITH IS NOT TO HAVE A

PERFECT KNOWLEDGE OF THINGS;

THEREFORE IF YE HAVE FAITH

YE HOPE FOR THINGS

WHICH ARE NOT SEEN,

which are true.

—ALMA 32:21

Whereby are given unto us

exceeding great and precious promises:

that by these ye might be partakers of the

divine nature,

having escaped the corruption

that is in the world through lust.

And beside this, giving all diligence,

add to your **FAITH** virtue

and to **VIRTUE** knowledge

and to **KNOWLEDGE** temperance

and to **TEMPERANCE** patience

and to **PATIENCE** godliness

and to **GODLINESS** brotherly kindness

and to **BROTHERLY KINDNESS** charity.

—2 Peter 1:4-7

KNOW YE NOT THAT

YE ARE THE TEMPLE OF GOD,

AND THAT THE SPIRIT OF GOD

DWELLETH IN YOU?

1 CORINTHIANS 3:16

Remember
the worth of souls is great
in the sight of God

—Doctrine & Covenants 18:10

for the Lord seeth
not as man seeth;

for man looketh
on the outward appearance,

but the Lord looketh on
the heart.

1 Samuel 16:7

If thou shalt ask, thou shalt receive

revelation upon *revelation*

knowledge upon *knowledge*

that thou mayest know the

mysteries and *peaceable things*

that which bringeth *joy*

that which bringeth *life eternal*

—Doctrine and Covenants 42:61

And as all have not
FAITH
SEEK *ye diligently*
& TEACH *one another*
words of wisdom;
yea, SEEK *ye out of the*

BEST BOOKS
words OF *wisdom;*

seek
even by LEARNING,
STUDY
& *also by*
FAITH.

Doctrine and Covenants 88:118

And if it seem evil unto you to serve the Lord,

choose you this day whom ye will serve;

WHETHER THE GODS WHICH YOUR FATHERS SERVED THAT WERE ON THE OTHER SIDE OF THE FLOOD, OR THE GODS OF THE AMORITES, IN WHOSE LAND YE DWELL:

but as for me and my house, WE WILL SERVE THE Lord

—JOSHUA 24:15

WHEREFORE, MEN ARE FREE ACCORDING TO THE FLESH; AND ALL THINGS ARE GIVEN THEM WHICH ARE EXPEDIENT UNTO MAN. **AND THEY ARE FREE TO CHOOSE LIBERTY & ETERNAL LIFE,** THROUGH THE **GREAT MEDIATOR** OF ALL MEN, OR TO CHOOSE **CAPTIVITY** AND **DEATH,** ACCORDING TO THE CAPTIVITY AND POWER OF THE DEVIL; FOR HE SEEKETH THAT ALL MEN MIGHT BE MISERABLE LIKE UNTO HIMSELF.

— 2 NEPHI 2:27

Therefore let your light so shine before this people, that they may see your good works and glorify your Father who is in heaven.

3 Nephi 12:16

AND LET US

NOT BE WEARY IN

WELL
DOING

FOR IN DUE SEASON

WE SHALL REAP,

IF WE FAINT

NOT.

GALATIONS 6:9

*M*y lips shall not

speak wickedness,

nor my tongue

utter deceit.

God forbid that

I should justify you:

till I die I will not remove mine integrity from me.

*M*y righteousness

I hold fast,

and will not let it go:

my heart shall

not reproach me

so long as I live.

Job 27:4-6

Therefore...
see that you are
merciful
unto your brethren;

deal **justly,**
judge **righteously,**

and

do good continually;

and if ye do all these things
then shall ye receive your reward

yea, ye shall have
mercy restored unto
you again;

ye shall
have **justice** restored unto
you again;

ye shall have a
righteous
judgement restored unto
you again;

and ye
shall have **good**
rewarded unto
you again.

— Alma 41:14

Who can find a virtuous woman? for her price is far above rubies.

Proverbs 31:10

If thou shalt ask, thou shalt receive

revelation upon *revelation*

knowledge upon *knowledge*

that thou mayest know the

mysteries and *peaceable things*

that which bringeth *joy*

that which bringeth *life eternal*

—Doctrine and Covenants 42:61

Let thy bowels
also be full of
charity
towards all men,
and to the household of faith,
and let
virtue
garnish thy thoughts unceasingly;
then shall thy confidence
wax strong in the
presence of God;
and the doctrine of the priesthood
shall distil upon thy soul
as the dews from
heaven.

Doctrine and Covenants 121:45

Therefore let your light so shine before this people, that they may see your good works and glorify your Father who is in heaven.

3 Nephi 12:16

FOR BEHOLD, THIS IS MY WORK AND MY GLORY— TO BRING TO PASS THE IMMORTALITY AND ETERNAL LIFE OF MAN.

–Moses 1:39

www.ingramcontent.com/pod-product-compliance
Lightning Source LLC
Chambersburg PA
CBHW040345060426